YOGA MUSIC
FOR PIANO SOLO
24 Chill Songs to Soothe Your Soul

ISBN 978-1-5400-3859-3

Visit Hal Leonard Online at
www.halleonard.com

World headquarters, contact:
Hal Leonard
7777 West Bluemound Road
Milwaukee, WI 53213
Email: info@halleonard.com

In Europe, contact:
Hal Leonard Europe Limited
1 Red Place
London, W1K 6PL
Email: info@halleonardeurope.com

In Australia, contact:
Hal Leonard Australia Pty. Ltd.
4 Lentara Court
Cheltenham, Victoria, 3192 Australia
Email: info@halleonard.com.au

ANGEL

Words and Music by
JACK JOHNSON

Moderately

BREATHE ME

Words and Music by DAN CAREY
and SIA KATE I. FURLER

CHASING CARS

Words and Music by GARY LIGHTBODY,
TOM SIMPSON, PAUL WILSON,
JONATHAN QUINN and NATHAN CONNOLLY

Moderately

COME AWAY WITH ME
from MAID IN MANHATTAN

Words and Music by
NORAH JONES

With pedal

DOWN

Words and Music by SAMANTHA GONGOL
and JEREMY LLOYD

Moderately slow groove

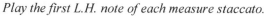

Play the first L.H. note of each measure staccato.

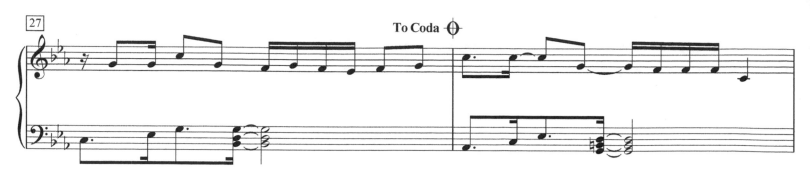

To Coda ⊕

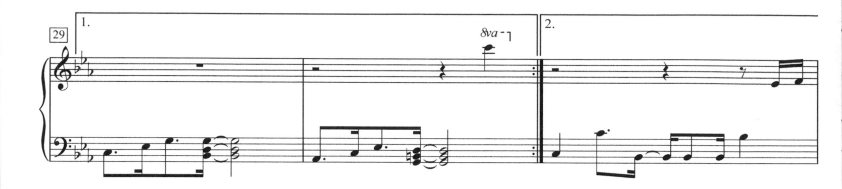

D.S. al Coda

CODA ⊕

HEY NOW

Words and Music by DANIEL ROTHMAN,
HANNAH REID and DOMINIC MAJOR

FIX YOU

Words and Music by GUY BERRYMAN,
JON BUCKLAND, WILL CHAMPION
and CHRIS MARTIN

HO HEY

Words and Music by JEREMY FRAITES
and WESLEY SCHULTZ

Moderately slow, in 2

With pedal

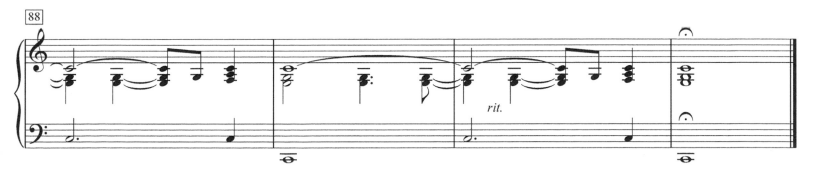

HOLOCENE

Words and Music by
JUSTIN VERNON

Moderate Folk, in 2

With pedal

28

I WILL FOLLOW YOU INTO THE DARK

Words and Music by
BENJAMIN GIBBARD

Moderately, in 2

IF YOU BELIEVE

Composed by
JIM BRICKMAN

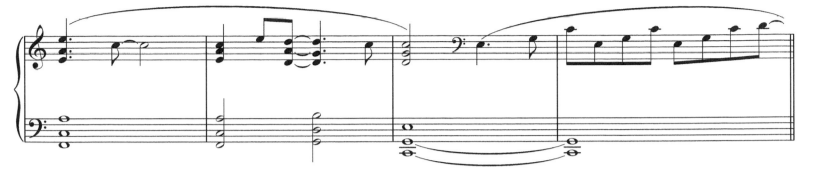

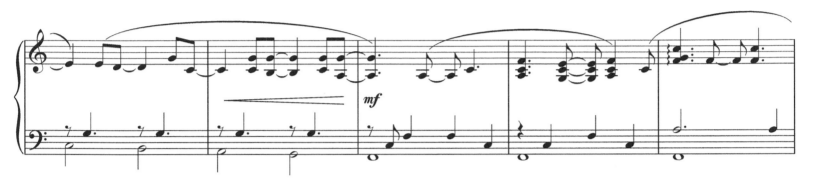

LET HER GO

Words and Music by
MICHAEL DAVID ROSENBERG

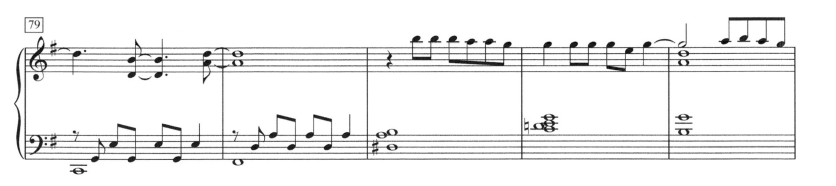

NEVER LET ME GO

Words and Muisc by FLORENCE WELCH,
THOMAS HULL and PAUL EPWORTH

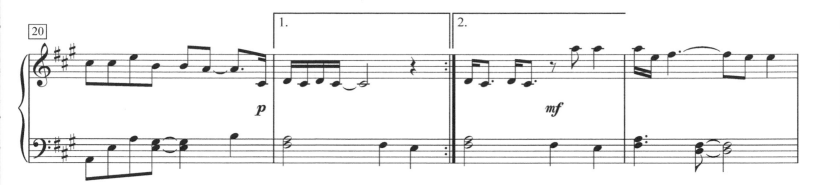

ROSLIN AND ADAMA

from the Universal Television Series BATTLESTAR GALACTICA

By BEAR McCREARY

Simple Folk feel

Pedal freely

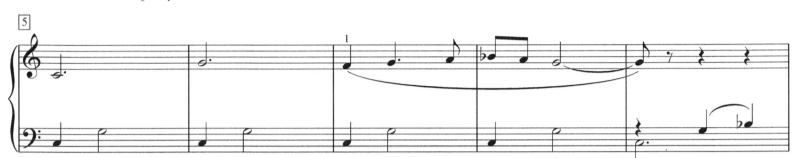

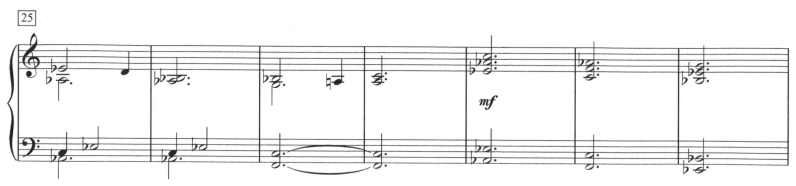

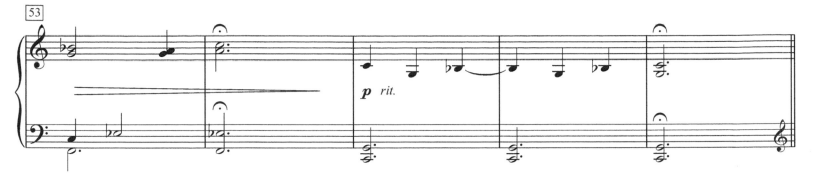

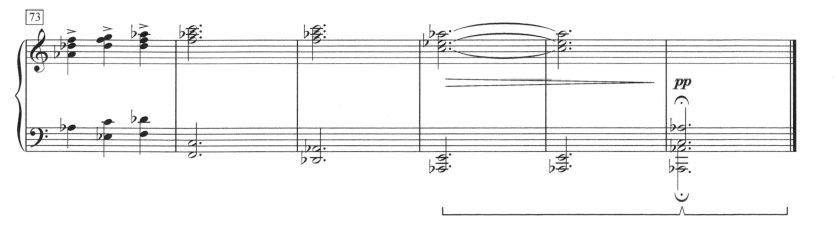

NOT ABOUT ANGELS
from the Motion Picture Soundtrack THE FAULT IN OUR STARS

Words and Music by
JASMINE VAN DEN BOGAERDE

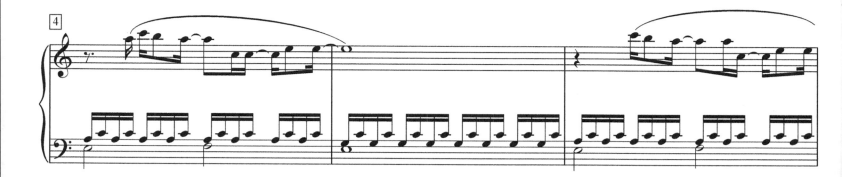

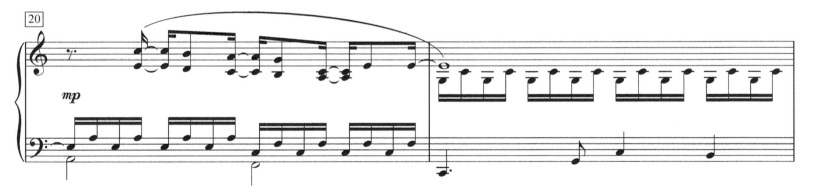

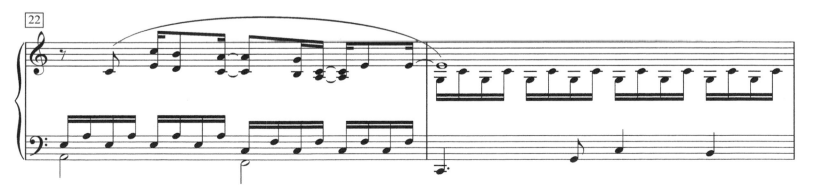

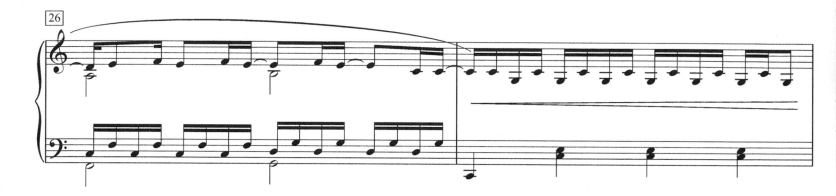

NUVOLE BIANCHE

Music by LUDOVICO EINAUDI

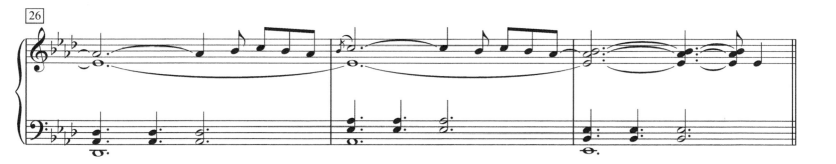

ORINOCO FLOW

Music by ENYA
Words by ROMA RYAN

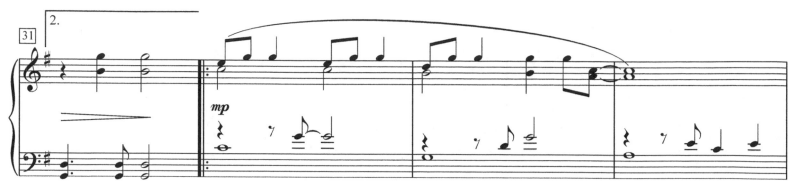

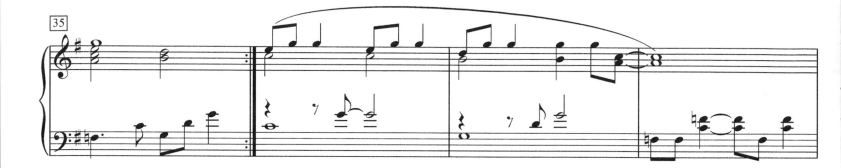

RETURN TO THE HEART

By DAVID LANZ

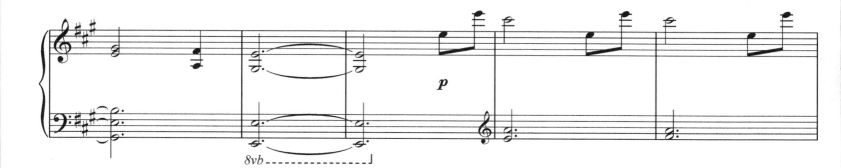

SUNRISE

Words and Music by NORAH JONES
and LEE ALEXANDER

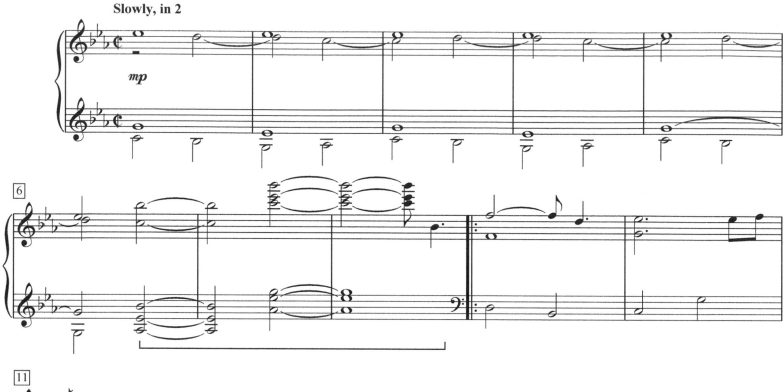

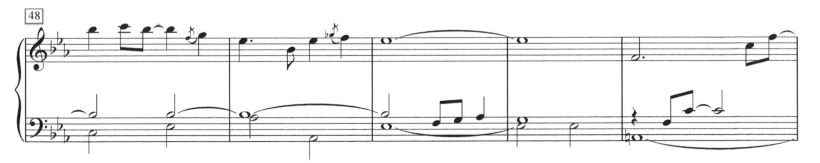

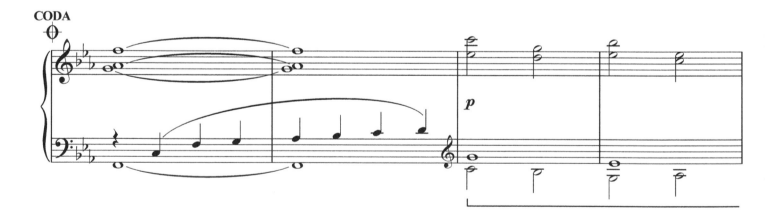

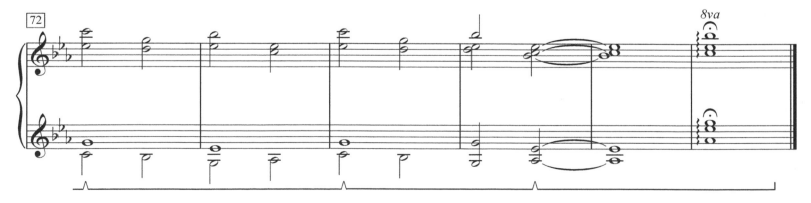

THIS YEAR'S LOVE

Words and Music by
DAVID GRAY

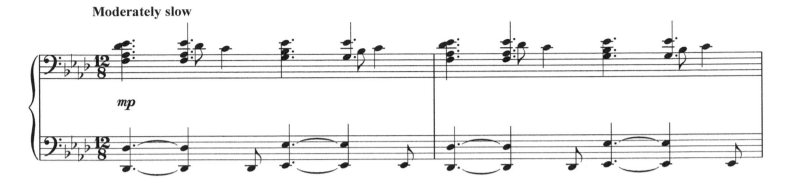

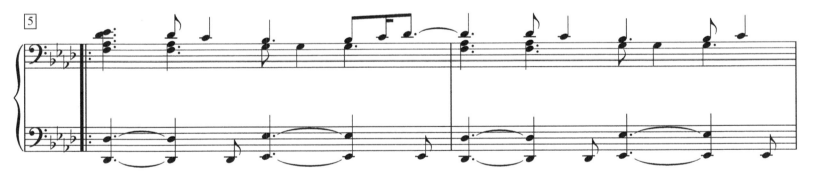

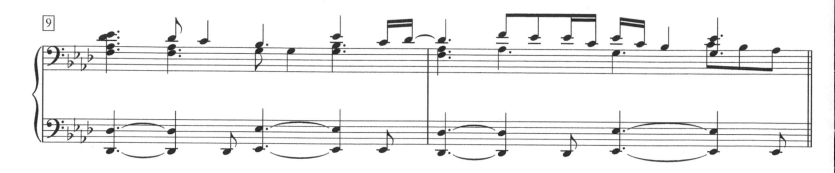

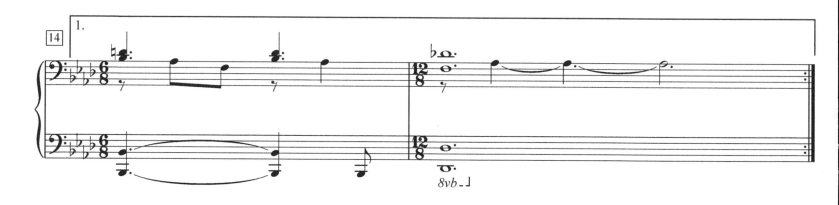

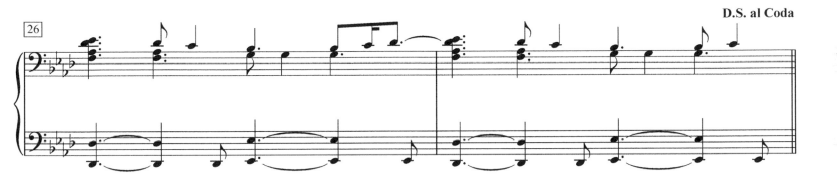

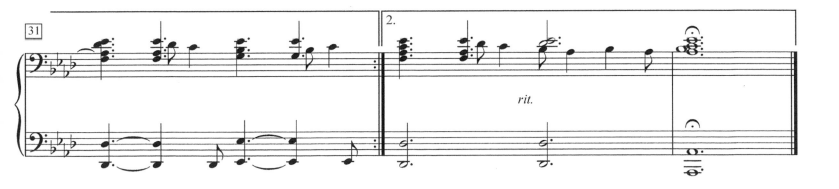

A THOUSAND YEARS

from the Summit Entertainment film THE TWILIGHT SAGA: BREAKING DAWN – Part 1

Words and Music by DAVID HODGES
and CHRISTINA PERRI

Moderately slow, in 1

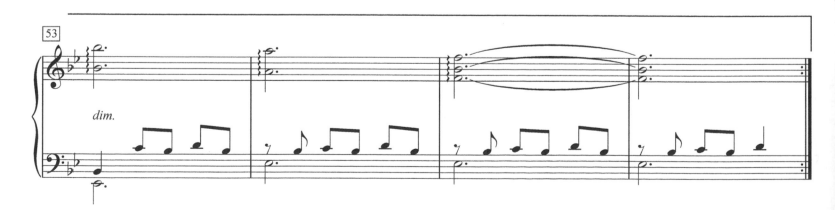

UNA MATTINA

Music by LUDOVICO EINAUDI

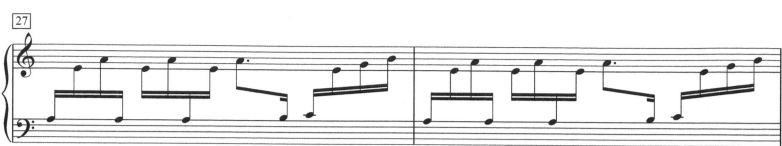

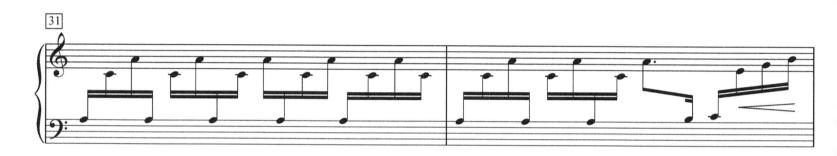

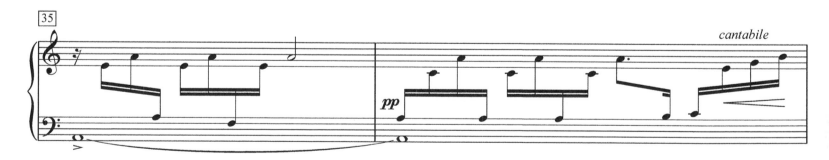

WATERMARK

Music by ENYA
Words by ROMA RYAN

Slowly, with rubato

WASH.

Words and Music by
JUSTIN VERNON

Steadily, in 2

With pedal, blurred

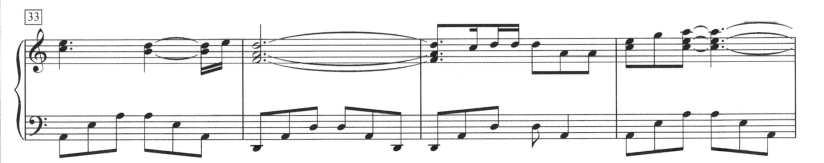

YOUR FAVORITE MUSIC ARRANGED FOR PIANO SOLO

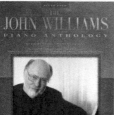

ARTIST, COMPOSER, TV & MOVIE SONGBOOKS

Adele for Piano Solo – 3rd Edition
00820186................... $19.99

The Beatles Piano Solo
00294023................... $17.99

A Charlie Brown Christmas
00313176................... $19.99

Paul Cardall – The Hymns Collection
00295925................... $24.99

Coldplay for Piano Solo
00307637................... $17.99

Selections from Final Fantasy
00148699................... $19.99

Alexis Ffrench – The Sheet Music Collection
00345258................... $19.99

Game of Thrones
00199166................... $19.99

Hamilton
00354612................... $19.99

Hillsong Worship Favorites
00303164................... $14.99

How to Train Your Dragon
00138210................... $22.99

Elton John Collection
00306040................... $24.99

La La Land
00283691................... $14.99

John Legend Collection
00233195................... $17.99

Les Misérables
00290271................... $22.99

Little Women
00338470................... $19.99

Outlander: The Series
00254460................... $19.99

The Peanuts® Illustrated Songbook
00313178................... $29.99

Astor Piazzolla – Piano Collection
00285510................... $19.99

Pirates of the Caribbean – Curse of the Black Pearl
00313256................... $22.99

Pride & Prejudice
00123854................... $17.99

Queen
00289784................... $19.99

John Williams Anthology
00194555................... $24.99

George Winston Piano Solos
00306822................... $22.99

MIXED COLLECTIONS

Beautiful Piano Instrumentals
00149926................... $19.99

Best Jazz Piano Solos Ever
00312079................... $24.99

Best Piano Solos Ever
00242928................... $22.99

Big Book of Classical Music
00310508................... $24.99

Big Book of Ragtime Piano
00311749................... $22.99

Christmas Medleys
00350572................... $16.99

Disney Medleys
00242588................... $19.99

Disney Piano Solos
00313128................... $17.99

Favorite Pop Piano Solos
00312523................... $16.99

Great Piano Solos
00311273................... $19.99

The Greatest Video Game Music
00201767................... $19.99

Most Relaxing Songs
00233879................... $19.99

Movie Themes Budget Book
00289137................... $14.99

100 of the Most Beautiful Piano Solos Ever
00102787................... $29.99

100 Movie Songs
00102804................... $32.99

Peaceful Piano Solos
00286009................... $19.99

Piano Solos for All Occasions
00310964................... $24.99

River Flows in You & Other Eloquent Songs
00123854................... $17.99

Sunday Solos for Piano
00311272................... $17.99

Top Hits for Piano Solo
00294635................... $16.99

HAL•LEONARD®

View songlists online and order from your favorite music retailer at

halleonard.com

1222
195

Prices, content, and availability subject to change without notice.

Disney characters and artwork TM & © 2021 Disney